Walking
Through
Grief
HIS Way

Faith-Based Healing for
the Heart That Is Hurtng

12-WEEK
GUIDED
WORKBOOK

Raynetta D. Bradley

ISBN:979-8-9871667-5-8

Publisher: HIS Way Inc.

CONTENTS

Introduction

"The Spirit of the Lord GOD is upon me; because the LORD hath anointed me to preach good tidings unto the meek; he hath sent me to bind up the brokenhearted, to proclaim liberty to the captives, and the opening of the prison to them that are bound; to proclaim the acceptable year of the LORD, and the day of vengeance of our God; to comfort all that mourn; to appoint unto them that mourn in Zion, to give unto them beauty for ashes, the oil of joy for mourning, the garment of praise for the spirit of heaviness; that they might be called trees of righteousness, the planting of the LORD, that he might be glorified" (Isaiah 61:1-3 KJV).

Grief is one of the most challenging paths we walk. Whether it's the loss of a loved one, a relationship, a dream, a job, or even a season of life, grief leaves a lasting mark. This workbook is a companion for that journey: a sacred space to reflect, cry, pray, and heal through the lens of faith.

God promises in Psalm 34:18, "The Lord is close to the brokenhearted and saves those who are crushed in spirit" (NIV). You are not alone in your mourning. As you walk through these 12 weeks, may you discover how to cope with loss, carry love forward, rediscover purpose, and find peace again. Healing is not forgetting, it is learning to live with love and hope again—HIS way.

What Is Faith-Based Grief?

Grief, from a faith-based perspective, is not just a psychological or emotional response to loss—it is a deeply human and sacred experience, intricately connected to our relationship with God.

Here are a few truths that shape how we can understand and walk through grief with faith:

- A Natural and Valid Response: Grief is an expression of love, not a sign of weakness or lack of faith.
- A Journey with Hope: In Christ, we grieve, but not without hope (1 Thessalonians 4:13).
- An Invitation to Faith: Grief can draw us closer to God, inviting us to trust Him with our pain.
- A Process of Transformation: Healing happens in layers, often with help from Scripture, prayer, and community.

IMPORTANT: Grief is unique for everyone. You may not be in the "listed" stage, and that's okay. Don't overcomplicate it. Instead, take a moment to sit with your feelings, pray, and invite the Holy Spirit to meet you where you are. Remember that grief isn't limited to the loss of a loved one; it can follow any significant loss—a relationship, a dream, a job, or even a season of life.

My Testimony

In this season—May 5, 2025, to be exact—I had an aha moment. It hit me that even in obedience, we grieve. As strange as it sounds, you can be praising and worshipping God and still be grieving. No one tells you that obedience to the Father and denying your flesh can lead you down a path of grief. No one tells you that surrendering your life to Christ can cause grief—or that even when you know you are doing what the LORD has called you to do, you can still experience grief.

Well, I'm here to tell you—it's true!

And I'm also here to tell you, as someone who has experienced grief on many levels, that your greatest weapon is praise!

Yes—had it not been for praise, thanksgiving, and having the heart of a worshipper, grief most likely would have taken me out. I've walked through seasons of being a single mother, betraying my body (the sacredness of who I am) to someone who was not my husband, imprisonment, being connected to the wrong people, getting shot, suffering partial paralysis, and being diagnosed with three autoimmune diseases. Not to mention financial lack. One time, I considered going to a shelter. I even asked the Lord, "Did You send me here to be homeless?" But despite it all, I never lost my praise.

Now, I'm writing this workbook, with the help and guidance of the Holy Spirit, so you too can know and experience peace, healing, deliverance, forgiveness, and freedom as you praise your way through your season of grief.

I can also testify: grieving does not equal depression. Depression is often the result of an unhealthy grieving process. There is a difference between a clinical diagnosis of depression and depression that results from an unhealthy grieving process, and that's the focus here. Be honest with yourself. Be gentle with yourself. You may or may not fully understand all the reasons you're grieving. For some, it may be one specific thing. For others, it could be a combination of experiences that have unpacked themselves in your soul and taken root in your heart.

I encourage you to ask the Holy Spirit to reveal what's there—what's in your heart, and what may be hindering forward movement in your life.

What is grieving your soul?

Receive. Acknowledge. Forgive.

Yes, forgive the offender—and even more importantly, forgive yourself—so that you can move forward healthy, whole, and healed.

As you journey through each week and each stage of grief, trust the Spirit of our risen Savior. Follow His lead, for He will take you deeper. This workbook is only a guide.

The healing of your soul is like peeling an onion—there are many layers before you get to the core. And at the center lies the part of you that's been buried beneath both pain and joy.

Now is the time to cut through the layers—and exchange the weight of heaviness for the weight of victorious glory.

Worship Playlist for Grief and Healing

Music is a powerful tool for comfort, hope, and worship. Consider listening to these songs as you work through each week, or whenever you need encouragement.

- Beauty for Ashes– Crystal Lewis
- Soaking In His Presence (Instrumental) – William Augusto
- Oceans (Where Feet May Fail) – Hillsong UNITED
- The Weight of Your Glory – Folabi Nuel
- You Say – Lauren Daigle
- Way Maker – Leeland
- It Is Well – Kristene DiMarco
- Blessings – Laura Story
- Praise You in This Storm – Casting Crowns
- Goodness of God – Bethel Music
- Broken Vessels (Amazing Grace) – Hillsong Worship
- Even If – Mercy Me

- Surrounded (Fight My Battles)– Michael W. Smith

Your Song Additions

Use the space below to add songs that speak to your heart in this season. These will become part of your personal soundtrack of healing.

_____

_____

_____

_____

_____

_____

_____

_____

_____

_____

_____

_____

_____

_____

_____

_____

_____

Opening Prayer
Before Starting This Journey

Heavenly Father,

I come before You with a heart that is broken, weary, and in need of Your healing touch. You are the God who binds up the brokenhearted and sets the captives free. I surrender this grief, this pain, and every burden I carry into Your loving hands.

Lord, I invite You into every room of my soul, into the places I've hidden, the wounds I've buried, and the memories that still hurt. Shine Your light into every corner and bring healing where there has been devastation.

By the authority given through Christ Jesus, I break agreement with sorrow that paralyzes, despair that overwhelms, and lies that tell me I won't recover. I declare that this grief will not define me, destroy me, or distance me from Your love.

Holy Spirit, be my Comforter and my Guide throughout this journey. Speak truth to every lie, bring peace to every storm, and stir hope where it has grown cold. Help me to grieve with You, not apart from You.

I receive Your peace, Your presence, and Your promises. I declare that healing is my portion, and freedom is my inheritance in Christ. Thank You, Father, for loving me through every stage of this journey. In Jesus' name, Amen.

Take a Moment

Write down how you feel after this prayer. Invite God into this very moment with you.

_____

_____

_____

_____

_____

_____

_____

_____

_____

_____

_____

Take three deep breaths—in through your nose, out through your mouth.

Do this before and after **each prompt, prayer, or activity**.

As you breathe, let go of what burdens you and receive the life-giving breath of God.

WEEK 1

SHOCK

"God is our refuge and strength, an ever-present help in trouble" (Psalm 46:1).

Theme: Feeling Numb – God Is Still Present

Grief Stage: Shock

What This Looks Like: Shock is a natural, immediate reaction to loss. It may feel like numbness, disbelief, or an inability to feel at all. This initial stage acts as a temporary buffer, protecting you from the full impact of the pain, allowing you to process the reality of the loss gradually.

Reflection Questions

What was your immediate reaction to your loss?

_____

_____

_____

_____

_____

_____

_____

_____

_____

_____

_____

Do you remember any physical or emotional sensations?

_____

_____

_____

_____

_____

_____

_____

_____

_____

_____

How have you sensed (or not sensed) God's presence?

_____

_____

_____

_____

_____

_____

_____

_____

_____

_____

_____

_____

Where were you?

_____

_____

_____

_____

_____

_____

_____

_____

_____

What did you see, feel, smell, taste, or hear?

_____

_____

_____

_____

_____

_____

_____

_____

_____

_____

Activity Prompt

Recall a moment today where you felt a flicker of God's presence, even if it was small. Write it down as a reminder that He is with you in this initial shock.

_____

_____

_____

_____

_____

_____

_____

_____

_____

Journaling Space

_____

_____

_____

_____

_____

_____

_____

_____

_____

_____

_____

_____

_____

_____

_____

_____

_____

_____

(Use this space to write freely. Be honest. God can handle it.)

Prayer Prompt

Dear God, I feel numb and unsure. Help me feel Your presence even when I don't feel anything else.

WEEK 2

DENIAL

"When you pass through the waters, I will be with you" (Isaiah 43:2).

Theme: When Reality Feels Too Heavy

Grief Stage: Denial

Why This Matters: Denial can be the mind's way of gently introducing us to a reality that feels too overwhelming to accept all at once. It provides a temporary shield, allowing us to process the loss at a pace we can manage. While it's a natural initial response, recognizing it helps us move toward accepting the truth of our loss in God's timing and with His support.

Reflection Questions

What behaviors or thoughts show you might be in denial?

_____

_____

_____

_____

_____

_____

_____

_____

_____

_____

_____

Are there moments when you pretend the loss didn't happen?

_____

_____

_____

_____

_____

_____

_____

_____

_____

_____

What would trusting God in this uncertainty look like?

_____

_____

_____

_____

_____

_____

_____

_____

_____

_____

_____

_____

_____

Activity Prompt

Reflect on a small, undeniable truth about your loss. Write it down and then spend a few moments in prayer acknowledging this reality to God.

_____

_____

_____

_____

_____

_____

_____

_____

_____

_____

_____

_____

_____

_____

Journaling Prompt

Write a letter to God expressing confusion, hesitation, and longing.

Prayer Prompt

God, when reality feels too heavy, meet me in my denial and gently lead me toward Your truth, one step at a time.

WEEK 3

YEARNING AND ANGER

"In your anger do not sin" (Ephesians 4:26).

Theme: God Can Handle My Honesty

Grief Stage: Yearning and Anger

What This Looks Like: Grief may bring deep longing for what was and intense anger toward yourself, others, or even God. These powerful emotions are a natural response to the pain of loss. Expressing them in a healthy way, rather than suppressing them, is crucial for healing and allows us to bring our full selves to God.

Reflection Questions

Who or what are you angry with?

_____

_____

_____

_____

_____

_____

_____

_____

_____

_____

_____

Rate your anger on a scale of 1–10.

☐ 1 – Calm and at peace—no anger present

☐ 2 – Slightly unsettled or mildly irritated

☐ 3 – Noticeable annoyance, but manageable

☐ 4 – Frustrated—beginning to feel tense

☐ 5 – Agitated—aware of emotional discomfort

☐ 6 – Angry—thoughts and body beginning to react

☐ 7 – Intensely angry—harder to stay composed

☐ 8 – Very angry—struggling to concentrate

☐ 9 – Overwhelmed by anger—close to outburst

☐ 10 – Explosive anger—at a breaking point

What scripture or song helps bring peace?

_____

_____

_____

_____

_____

_____

_____

_____

_____

_____

_____

_____

Activity Prompt

Write out what you would say to the person or situation connected to your grief. You don't have to send it, but the act of expressing these feelings can be cathartic.

_____

_____

_____

_____

_____

_____

_____

_____

_____

_____

_____

_____

_____

_____

Journal Prompt

What are you holding inside that you need to honestly bring before God today?

_____

_____

_____

_____

_____

_____

_____

_____

_____

_____

_____

_____

Prayer Prompt

Lord, I'm angry. I'm tired. I don't understand. Please help me hand this anger over to You.

WEEK 4

EMOTIONAL DESPAIR AND SADNESS

"The Lord is close to the brokenhearted and saves those who are crushed in spirit" (Psalm 34:18).

Theme: God Is Near to the Brokenhearted

Grief Stage: Emotional Despair and Sadness

Why This Matters: This stage brings deep emotional pain, often sadness, isolation, or hopelessness. Allowing ourselves to feel this deeply, while incredibly painful, is a necessary part of acknowledging the profound impact of our loss and leaning into God's comfort. It's a testament to the love we had and the value of what we've lost.

Reflection Questions

What emotions are surfacing now?

_____

_____

_____

_____

_____

_____

_____

_____

_____

_____

Are there specific memories that bring deep sadness?

_____

_____

_____

_____

_____

_____

_____

_____

_____

_____

What comfort have you found in scripture or prayer?

_____

_____

_____

_____

_____

_____

_____

_____

_____

_____

_____

_____

Activity Prompt

Find a quiet space and allow yourself to feel the sadness fully for a set period. Afterward, read Psalm 34:18 aloud and invite God's nearness.

Journaling Prompt

Write your emotions as a raw conversation with God. Don't edit yourself. Just write.

_____

_____

_____

_____

_____

_____

_____

_____

_____

_____

_____

_____

_____

_____

_____

Prayer Prompt

Lord, in my sorrow and despair, remind me that You are near—holding every tear, hearing every cry, and healing my heart with Your presence.

CHECK-IN: REFLECTION AFTER WEEK 4

What has changed in your emotions or faith since starting this workbook?

_____

_____

_____

_____

_____

_____

_____

_____

_____

_____

Which scripture, prayer, or activity has brought you the most comfort?

_____

_____

_____

_____

_____

_____

_____

_____

_____

_____

_____

What is one thing you want to ask God for in the coming weeks?

_____

_____

_____

_____

_____

_____

_____

_____

_____

Write a short prayer or affirmation for yourself.

_____

_____

_____

_____

_____

WEEK 5

SUFFERING

"Our present sufferings are not worth comparing with the glory that will be revealed in us" (Romans 8:18).

Theme: Sitting in the Pain with God

Grief Stage: Suffering

What This Looks Like: This is the prolonged ache of loss, the period when sorrow seems to linger. It often includes guilt, regret, or longing that feels like it won't go away. Acknowledging this persistent pain and bringing it to God allows Him to meet us in our vulnerability and offer solace.

Reflection Questions

How would you describe your suffering during this time?

_____

_____

_____

_____

_____

_____

_____

_____

_____

_____

_____

What helps you survive these long, painful moments?

_____

_____

_____

_____

_____

_____

_____

_____

_____

Have you felt guilt or regret? If so, what about?

_____

_____

_____

_____

_____

_____

_____

_____

_____

_____

_____

_____

Activity Prompt

Write a list of things you wish others understood about your grief. Share one of these with a trusted friend or in your journal to give voice to your experience.

_____

_____

_____

_____

_____

_____

_____

_____

_____

_____

Journaling Prompt

Invite God into this ache. Write a raw prayer or reflection describing how it feels to suffer and what you need from Him now.

_____

_____

_____

_____

_____

_____

_____

_____

_____

_____

_____

Prayer Prompt

Lord, meet me in the ache I can't escape, and sit with me in the sorrow I can't yet heal.

WEEK 6

REORGANIZATION AND ADJUSTING TO CHANGE

"There is a time for everything, and a season for every activity under the heavens" (Ecclesiastes 3:1).

Theme: Small Steps, New Rhythms

Grief Stage: Reorganization

Why This Matters: This stage involves slowly adapting to life after loss. It's not about "getting over it," but learning how to live differently, carrying your grief and faith together. Recognizing the small steps we take and the new routines we establish helps us see God's hand in guiding us toward a new normal.

Reflection Questions

What small steps have you taken toward healing?

_____

_____

_____

_____

_____

_____

_____

_____

_____

_____

What does "moving forward" mean to you personally?

_____

_____

_____

_____

_____

_____

_____

_____

_____

_____

_____

What encourages or inspires you now, no matter how small?

_____

_____

_____

_____

_____

_____

_____

_____

_____

_____

_____

_____

Activity Prompt

Make a list: What new routines or habits are forming in your life?

_____

_____

_____

_____

_____

_____

_____

_____

Which ones are helping you feel stronger? Thank God for these small signs of progress.

_____

_____

_____

_____

_____

_____

_____

_____

_____

Journaling Prompt

Reflect on how God is helping you reorganize your life. Has anything surprised you? Encouraged you?

_____

_____

_____

_____

_____

_____

_____

_____

_____

_____

_____

Prayer Prompt

Lord, help me embrace the small steps and new rhythms, trusting that You are gently leading me into life beyond the loss.

WEEK 7

LETTING GO AND FINDING MEANING

"Forget the former things; do not dwell on the past. See, I am doing a new thing!" (Isaiah 43:18-19).

Theme: Releasing Without Forgetting

Grief Stage: Letting Go and Purpose

What This Looks Like: Letting go does not mean forgetting. It means releasing the pain and making space for new meaning and purpose.

Reflection Questions

What are you afraid to let go of?

_____

_____

_____

_____

_____

_____

_____

_____

_____

_____

_____

What memories do you want to hold onto?

_____

_____

_____

_____

_____

_____

_____

_____

_____

_____

_____

How might God use your story for good?

_____

_____

_____

_____

_____

_____

_____

_____

_____

_____

_____

Activity Prompt

Create a "memory box" or journal page for treasured memories. Pray for courage to release what you cannot carry.

Journaling Prompt

What pain are you ready to release so you can make room for healing and purpose?

_____

_____

_____

_____

_____

_____

_____

_____

Prayer Prompt

God, help me release what I cannot change and trust You for new meaning.

WEEK 8

ACCEPTANCE AND SURRENDER

"Not my will, but Yours be done" (Luke 22:42).

Theme: Embracing What Is

Grief Stage: Acceptance and Surrender

Why This Matters: Acceptance is not approval of loss, but surrendering to God's will and trusting His plan.

Reflection Questions

What does acceptance look like for you?

_____

_____

_____

_____

_____

_____

_____

_____

_____

_____

_____

_____

_____

Where do you still struggle to surrender?

_____

_____

_____

_____

_____

_____

_____

_____

_____

_____

_____

Activity Prompt

Write a prayer of surrender, naming what you are releasing to God.

_____

_____

_____

_____

_____

_____

_____

_____

_____

_____

_____

_____

Journaling Prompt

Describe a moment when you felt God's peace in surrender.

_____

_____

_____

_____

_____

_____

_____

_____

_____

_____

_____

_____

Prayer Prompt

Lord, help me let go of what I cannot change and find peace in trusting what You allow.

CHECK-IN: REFLECTION AFTER WEEK 8

What progress do you notice in your journey?

_____

_____

_____

_____

_____

_____

_____

_____

_____

Which activities or prayers have helped you most?

_____

_____

_____

_____

_____

_____

_____

_____

What new questions or hopes are emerging?

_____

_____

_____

_____

_____

_____

_____

_____

Write a prayer of gratitude for how far you have come.

_____

_____

_____

_____

_____

_____

_____

_____

WEEK 9

GRATITUDE AND PRAISE

"Give thanks in all circumstances; for this is God's will for you in Christ Jesus" (1 Thessalonians 5:18).

Theme: Worship in the Wilderness

Grief Stage: Gratitude & Praise

What This Looks Like: Gratitude doesn't ignore pain but chooses to see God's goodness even in the wilderness.

Reflection Questions

What can you thank God for right now?

_____

_____

_____

_____

_____

_____

_____

_____

_____

_____

_____

_____

How has praise helped you in your grief?

_____

_____

_____

_____

_____

_____

_____

_____

_____

_____

Activity Prompt

Make a gratitude list. Sing or listen to a worship song that lifts your spirit.

_____

_____

_____

_____

_____

_____

_____

_____

_____

Journal Prompt

Write down how you can worship God today, even in the midst of your pain.

_____

_____

_____

_____

_____

_____

_____

_____

_____

_____

_____

_____

Prayer Prompt

Lord, help me praise You even in my pain.

WEEK 10

FORGIVENESS AND RELEASE

"Be kind and compassionate to one another, forgiving each other, just as in Christ God forgave you" (Ephesians 4:32).

Theme: Freedom Through Forgiveness

Grief Stage: Forgiveness and Release

What This Looks Like: Forgiveness is a gift you give yourself. It frees you from bitterness and opens the door to healing.

Reflection Questions

Who do you need to forgive (including yourself)?

_____

_____

_____

_____

_____

_____

_____

_____

_____

_____

_____

What's holding you back from forgiveness?

_____

_____

_____

_____

_____

_____

_____

_____

Activity Prompt

Write a letter of forgiveness (You don't have to send it).

_____

_____

_____

_____

_____

_____

_____

_____

_____

Journal Prompt

Write down how you feel after writing the letter, and what you sense God is saying to you.

_____

_____

_____

_____

_____

_____

_____

_____

_____

_____

_____

_____

_____

_____

Prayer Prompt

God, give me the strength to forgive and release all that holds me back.

WEEK 11

HOPE AND NEW VISION

"For I know the plans I have for you" (Jeremiah 29:11).

Theme: Looking Forward with Faith

Grief Stage: Hope and Vision

What This Looks Like: Hope is daring to believe in God's good future, even when you can't see it yet.

Reflection Questions

What dreams or hopes are stirring in your heart?

_____

_____

_____

_____

_____

_____

_____

_____

_____

How can you trust God with your future?

_____

_____

_____

_____

_____

_____

_____

_____

_____

Activity Prompt

Write down one hope or goal for the future. Pray over it and ask God to guide you.

_____

_____

_____

_____

_____

_____

_____

_____

_____

Journal Prompt

Write down what it means for you to have faith when you can't see what's ahead.

_____

_____

_____

_____

_____

_____

_____

_____

_____

_____

_____

Prayer Prompt

Lord, help me look ahead with faith, trusting in the goodness You've prepared—even when I can't yet see the way.

WEEK 12

LIVING WITH LOSS AND LOVE

"Weeping may endure for a night, but joy comes in the morning" (Psalm 30:5).

Theme: Carrying Grief and Joy Together

Grief Stage: Living with Loss and Love

What This Looks Like: You can carry grief and joy together. This is the journey of living with loss but also with love, hope, and purpose.

Reflection Questions

How has your understanding of grief changed?

_____

_____

_____

_____

_____

_____

_____

_____

_____

_____

_____

What does it look like to live with both loss and love?

_____

_____

_____

_____

_____

_____

_____

_____

Activity Prompt

Plan a small act of kindness or service in honor of your loved one or what you've lost.

Journal Prompt

Write down how you feel at the end of this 12-week journey.

_____

_____

_____

_____

_____

_____

_____

_____

_____

_____

_____

_____

_____

_____

_____

_____

Prayer Prompt

Thank You, God, for teaching me how to live with loss and love. Help me walk forward in hope.

FINAL CHECK-IN: REFLECTION AFTER WEEK 12

What has God shown you about yourself during this journey?

_____

_____

_____

_____

_____

_____

_____

_____

What are you grateful for, even in your grief?

_____

_____

_____

_____

_____

_____

_____

_____

How will you continue to seek healing and hope?

_____

_____

_____

_____

_____

_____

_____

_____

_____

Write a closing prayer for your journey.

_____

_____

_____

_____

_____

_____

_____

_____

_____

MOVING FORWARD IN HOPE

As you complete this 12-week journey, remember: Grief is not something you "finish"—it's something you learn to carry, with God's help. You are not alone. God's love, comfort, and purpose are with you always.

Closing Prayer

Heavenly Father,

Thank You for walking with me through every valley and every stage of grief. I trust that You will continue to comfort, guide, and restore me. Help me to carry forward the love I have lost, to find meaning in my pain, and to live with hope and faith. In Jesus' name. Amen.

 **Final Tips**

1. Be gentle with yourself: Healing is not linear.
2. Repeat sections as needed: Some weeks may require more time.
3. Reach out for help: Use the resources page if you need extra support.
4. Celebrate progress: Every small step is a victory.
5. Keep worshipping: Let praise be your anchor.

ABOUT THE AUTHOR & SUPPORT

Raynetta D. Bradley, MBA, BA, CFLE

As a certified Biblical Counselor, Certified Family Life Educator (CFLE), and Life Coach, I am honored to walk alongside you on this journey. My calling is to help, inspire and serve others on their path to health, wholeness, and healing through faith-based counseling and practical support.

For support, prayer, or coaching:

Email: info@walkingthroughgriefhisway.com

Website: http://walkingthroughgriefhisway.com/

Phone: 470-887-0940

Other Books by the Author

Walking Through Grief His Way – Companion Guide

Walking Through Grief His Way – Facilitator's Guide

Journey to Peace and Love: Experiencing Peace and Love in a World of Chaos

The Devil Thought He Had Me: A Story of Supernatural Deliverance

Support Hotlines

National Suicide Prevention Lifeline: 1-800-273-8255

SAMHSA Helpline: 1-800-662-HELP (4357)

Notes

Notes

Notes

Made in the USA
Middletown, DE
18 November 2025

21799006R00043